Presented To:

From:

_____

Date:

_____

JOY TO THE WORLD

Honor Books
Tulsa, Oklahoma

Compiled by Lisa Hughes.

Joy to the World

ISBN 1-56292-936-4

Copyright © 2002 by Honor Books

P.O. Box 55388

Tulsa, Oklahoma 74155

Introduction

Christmas is a time of joy. Our carols call us to rejoice. Our Christmas cards are covered with such cheerful words as "Merry Christmas," "Joy to the World," and "Happy Holidays." Something about the holiday season stirs up joyful emotions; and the reason that we celebrate causes us to overflow in acts of charity, hospitality, and generosity.

This book will give you even more to be joyful about by sharing the joys of yesterday, tomorrow's hope of eternity, and suggestions to make this present-day Christmas a joyful time. You will enjoy reading the Christmas carols and quotations from the past about Christmas joy. The trivia we have included will show you how Christmas joy looked in the past, while the recipes and suggestions will help you to make this present Christmas one of the most joyful.

Sit back in your most comfortable chair with something hot to chase the winter chill away and revel in Christmas joy!

Contents

Joy to the World

Joy to the world, the Lord is come!
Let earth receive her King;
Let every heart prepare Him room,
And heaven and nature sing,
And heaven and nature sing,
And heaven, and heaven, and nature sing.

Joy to the world, the Savior reigns!
Let men their songs employ;
While fields and floods, rocks, hills and plains
Repeat the sounding joy,
Repeat the sounding joy,
Repeat, repeat, the sounding joy.

No more let sins and sorrows grow,
Nor thorns infest the ground;
He comes to make His blessings flow
Far as the curse is found,
Far as the curse is found,
Far as, far as, the curse is found.

He rules the world with truth and grace,
And makes the nations prove
The glories of His righteousness,
And wonders of His love,
And wonders of His love,
And wonders, wonders, of His love.

ISAAC WATTS

*My soul glorifies the Lord
and my spirit rejoices
in God my Savior.*

LUKE 1:46-47

WORDS OF
CHRISTMAS JOY

"Christmas Everywhere"

Everywhere, everywhere, Christmas tonight!
Christmas in lands of the fir-tree and pine,
Christmas in lands of the palm-tree and vine,
Christmas where snow peaks stand solemn and white,
Christmas where cornfields stand sunny and bright.
Christmas where children are hopeful and gay,
Christmas where old men are patient and gray,
Christmas where peace, like a dove in his flight,
Broods o'er brave men in the thick of the fight;
Everywhere, everywhere, Christmas tonight!
For the Christ-Child who comes is the Master of all;
No palace too great, no cottage too small.

PHILLIPS BROOKS

A Matter of Joy

It is a matter of joy to think that God has sent the message of grace to so many millions, by the wide spread of his gospel.

MATTHEW HENRY

"The Little Mud-Sparrows" (excerpt)

Our souls are like the sparrows
Imprisoned in the clay,
Bless Him who came to give them wings
Upon a Christmas Day!

ELIZABETH STUART PHELPS

*She [Mary] will give birth to a son,
and you are to give him the name Jesus,
because he will save his people from their sins.*

MATTHEW 1:21

14

Even Before He Came

Even before her travail, prophets danced for joy,
and women foretold what was to come, and John,
when he had not yet come forth from the belly,
leaped from the very womb.

JOHN CHRYSOSTOM

No Room for the Coming of Joy

In those days Caesar Augustus issued a decree that a census should be taken of the entire Roman world. . . .

So Joseph also went up from the town of Nazareth in Galilee to Judea, to Bethlehem the town of David, because he belonged to the house and line of David. He went there to register with Mary, who was pledged to be married to him and was expecting a child. While they were there, the time came for the baby to be born, and she gave birth to her firstborn, a son. She wrapped him in cloths and placed him in a manger, because there was no room for them in the inn.

LUKE 2:1,4-7

"That Holy Thing"

They all were looking for a king
To slay their foes and lift them high:
Thou cam'st, a little baby thing
That made a woman cry.

GEORGE MACDONALD

The Joy of the Magi

After Jesus was born in Bethlehem in Judea, during the time of King Herod, Magi from the east came to Jerusalem and asked, "Where is the one who has been born king of the Jews? We saw his star in the east and have come to worship him."

. . . they went on their way, and the star they had seen in the east went ahead of them until it stopped over the place where the child was. When they saw the star, they were overjoyed. On coming to the house, they saw the child with his mother Mary, and they bowed down and worshiped him. Then they opened their treasures and presented him with gifts of gold and of incense and of myrrh.

MATTHEW 2:1-2,9-11

My Only Tribute!

And now kneel I in prayer hard by
The cradle of the Child to-day;
Nor crown, nor robe, nor spice I bring
As offering unto Christ, my King.

Yet have I brought a gift the Child
May not despise, however small;
For here I lay my heart to-day,
And it is full of love to all.
Take Thou the poor but loyal thing,
My only tribute, Christ, my King!

EUGENE FIELD
EXCERPT FROM "THE THREE KINGS OF COLOGNE"

The Gifts of the Magi

The three Wise Men were named Melchior, Caspar, and Balthasar. Melchior presented a casket of gold to the infant Christ; this symbolized the King He was to become. Caspar brought myrrh, a symbolic gift for a great Physician. Balthasar brought frankincense, a gift suitable for a high Priest.

A Hymn Sung as by the Shepherds

Welcome, all wonders in one sight!
Eternity shut in a span!
Summer in winter, day in night!
Heaven in earth, and God in man!
Great little One! Whose all-embracing birth
Lifts earth to heaven, stoops heaven to earth. . . .

To Thee, meek Majesty! soft King
Of simple graces and sweet loves:
Each of us his lamb will bring,
Each his pair of silver doves;
Till burnt at last in fire of Thy fair eyes,
Ourselves become our own best sacrifice.

RICHARD CRASHAW

News of Great Joy

There were shepherds living out in the fields nearby, keeping watch over their flocks at night. An angel of the Lord appeared to them, and the glory of the Lord shone around them, and they were terrified. But the angel said to them, "Do not be afraid. I bring you good news of great joy that will be for all the people. Today in the town of David a Savior has been born to you; he is Christ the Lord. This will be a sign to you: You will find a baby wrapped in cloths and lying in a manger."

Suddenly a great company of the heavenly host appeared with the angel, praising God and saying,

"Glory to God in the highest, and on earth peace to men on whom his favor rests."

LUKE 2:8-14

Christmas in the Heart

The only real blind person at Christmastime
is he who has not Christmas in his heart.

HELEN KELLER

Strange World

"It was the seven hundred fifty-third year since the founding of Rome. Gaius Julius Caesar Octavianus Augustus was living in a palace of the Palatine Hill, busily engaged upon the task of ruling his empire.

"In a little village of distant Syria, Mary the wife of Joseph the Carpenter, was tending her little boy, born in a stable of Bethlehem.

"This is a strange world. Before long the palace and the stable were to meet in open combat. And the stable was to emerge victorious."

HENDRIK WILLEM VAN LOON, *THE STORY OF MANKIND*

Unto Us a Son Is Given

Given, not lent,
And not withdrawn, once sent,
This Infant of mankind, this One,
Is still the little welcome Son.

New every year,
New-born and newly dear,
He comes with tidings and a song,
The ages long, the ages long.

Even as the cold
Keen winter grows not old,
As childhood is so fresh, forseen,
And spring in the familiar green.

Sudden as sweet
Come the expected feet.
All joy is young, and new all art,
And He, too, whom we have by heart.

ALICE MEYNELL

Grief Turn'd to Joy!

Now, death is life! And grief is turn'd to joy!
Since glory shone on that auspicious morn,
When God incarnate came, not to destroy,
But man to save and manhood's state adorn!

W. F. DAWSON

26

Christmas

The earth has grown old with its burden of care
But at Christmas it always is young,
The heart of the jewel burns lustrous and fair
And its soul full of music breaks forth on the air,
When the song of the angels is sung.

The feet of the humblest may walk in the field
Where the feet of the holiest have trod,
This, this is the marvel to mortals revealed
When the silvery trumpets of Christmas have pealed,
That mankind are children of God.

PHILLIPS BROOKS

Bethlehem Town

There burns a star o'er Bethlehem town—See, O my eyes!
And gloriously it beameth down
Upon a virgin mother meek
And Him whom solemn Magi seek.
Burn on, O star! And be the light
To guide us all to Him this night!

The angels walk in Bethlehem town—Hush, O my heart!
The angels come and bring a crown
To Him, our Saviour and our King;
And sweetly all this night they sing.
Sing on in rapturous angel throng,
That we may learn that heavenly song!

Near Bethlehem town there blooms a tree—O heart, beat low!
And it shall stand on Calvary!
But from the shade thereof we turn
Unto the start that still shall burn
When Christ is dead and risen again
To mind us that He died for men.

There is a cry in Bethlehem town—Hark, O my soul!
'Tis of the Babe that wears the crown.
It telleth us that man is free—
That He redeemeth all and me!
The night is sped—behold the morn!
Sing, O my soul; The Christ is born!

EUGENE FIELD

Christmas Hymn (excerpt)

Sing, O my heart!
Sing thou in rapture this dear morn
Whereon the blessed Prince is born!
And as thy songs shall be of love,
So let my deeds be charity—
By the dear Lord that reigns above,
By Him that died upon the tree,
By this fair morn
Whereon is born
The Christ that saveth all and me!

EUGENE FIELDS

Old Fashioned Joy from Noah Webster

JOY, n.

The passion or emotion excited by the acquisition or expectation of good; that excitement of pleasurable feelings which is caused by success, good fortune, the gratification of desire or some good possessed, or by a rational prospect of possessing what we love or desire; gladness; exultation; exhilaration of spirits.

WEBSTER'S 1828 *DICTIONARY OF AMERICAN ENGLISH*

Christmas Joy for the Poor

When other Sins grow old by Time,
Then Avarice is in its prime,
Yet feed the Poor at Christmas time.

POOR RICHARD'S ALMANACK, DECEMBER, 1757

*A generous man will himself be blessed,
for he shares his food with the poor.*

PROVERBS 22:9

A Christmas Hymn

The night that before no name had worn,
To it a happy name is given;
For in that stable lay new-born
The peaceful Prince of Earth and Heaven,
In the solemn midnight centuries ago.

ALFRED DOMETT

Christmas Morning

The angel host that sped last night,
Bearing the wondrous news afar,
Came in their ever-glorious flight
Unto a slumbering little star.

"Awake and sing, 0 star!" they cried.
"Awake and glorify the morn!
Herald the tidings far and wide
He that shall lead His flock is born!"

The little star awoke and sung
As only stars in rapture may,
And presently where church bells hung
The joyous tidings found their way.

"Awake, 0 bells! 'Tis Christmas morn—
Awake and let thy music tell
To all mankind that now is born
What Shepherd loves His lambkins well!"

Then rang the bells as fled the night
O'er dreaming land and drowsing deep,
And coming with the morning light,
They called, my child, to you asleep.

Sweetly and tenderly they spoke,
And lingering round your little bed,
Their music pleaded till you woke,
And this is what their music said:

"Awake and sing! 'Tis Christmas
   morn,
Whereon all earth salutes her King!
In Bethlehem is the Shepherd born.
Awake, 0 little lamb, and sing!"

So, dear my child, kneel at my feet,
And with those voices from above
Share thou this holy time with me,
The universal hymn of love.

EUGENE FIELD

*Forget, forgive, for who may say
that Christmas day may ever come
to host or guest again.*

WILLIAM HENRY HARRISON MURRAY

A Kind, Forgiving Time

I have always thought of Christmas-time, when it has come round, as a good time: a kind, forgiving, charitable, pleasant time: the only time I know of in the long calendar of the year, when men and women seem by one consent to open their shut-up hearts freely, and to think of people. . . . And therefore, though it has never put a scrap of gold or silver in my pocket, I believe that it has done me good, and will do me good, and I say, God bless it!

CHARLES DICKENS, *A CHRISTMAS CAROL*

Feast Thy Needy Neighbors

Now that the time has come
wherein Our Saviour Christ was born,
The larder's full of beef and pork,
The granary's full of corn.
As God hath plenty to thee sent,
Take comfort of thy labors,
And let it never thee repent,
To feast thy needy neighbors.

POOR ROBIN'S ALMANACK, 1700

"*Freely you have received, freely give.*"

MATTHEW 10:8

Give and spend, and God will send.

OLD PROVERB

*"Give, and it shall be given unto you; good measure, pressed
down, and shaken together, and running over, shall men give
into your bosom. For with the same measure that ye mete
withal it shall be measured to you again."*

LUKE 6:38 KJV

39

Song

Why do the bells of Christmas ring?
Why do little children sing?
Once a lovely shining star,
Seen by shepherds from afar,
Gently moved until its light
Made a manger's cradle bright.

There a darling baby lay,
Pillowed soft upon the hay,
And its mother sang and smiled:
"This is Christ, the Holy Child!"
Therefore the bells for Christmas ring,
Therefore little children sing.

EUGENE FIELD

Either Way It's Christmas!

At Christmas, play and make good cheer,
For Christmas comes but once a year.

THOMAS TUSSER
EXCERPT FROM *A FARMER'S DAILY DIET*

I will honor Christmas in my heart,
and try to keep it all the year.

CHARLES DICKENS, A CHRISTMAS CAROL

The angel said unto them,
Fear not: for, behold,
I bring you good tidings of great joy,
which shall be to all people.

LUKE 2:10 KJV

JOYFUL CHRISTMAS
CAROLS

Singing Psalm 98

Isaac Watts (1674-1748), the writer of the lyrics to "Joy to the World," began as a pastor of an independent church in England. He published this joyous Christmas carol in 1719 after a time of ill health had forced him to leave the ministry.

Watts included "Joy to the World" as a paraphrase of Psalm 98 for people to sing in his collection, *The Psalms of David Imitated in the Language of the New Testament.*

Handel's Messiah *and* Joy to the World

The tune to "Joy to the World" is the piecing together of themes in Handel's *Messiah* found in the chorus and in the instrumental interludes in "Lift up your heads" in addition to the introduction and interludes of the recitative "Comfort ye."

This tune was popularized by Lowell Mason in the United States under the title "Antioch." Antioch is the city in Syria where believers were first called Christians.

Joy to the World Psalm

1 O sing unto the LORD a new song; for he hath done marvellous things: his right hand, and his holy arm, hath gotten him the victory.

2 The LORD hath made known his salvation: his righteousness hath he openly shewed in the sight of the heathen.

3 He hath remembered his mercy and his truth toward the house of Israel: all the ends of the earth have seen the salvation of our God.

4 Make a joyful noise unto the LORD, all the earth: make a loud noise, and rejoice, and sing praise.

5 Sing unto the LORD with the harp; with the harp, and the voice of a psalm.

6 With trumpets and sound of cornet make a joyful noise before the LORD, the King.

7 Let the sea roar, and the fulness thereof; the world, and they that dwell therein.

8 Let the floods clap *their* hands: let the hills be joyful together

9 Before the LORD; for he cometh to judge the earth: with righteousness shall he judge the world, and the people with equity.

PSALM 98 KJV

An Almost-Lost Tradition

The Christmas carol was initially created in the form of a well-understood song about the Nativity. That tradition disappeared for some time. In 1822, Davies Gilbert published *A Collection and Christmas Carols,* and the tradition of caroling was renewed.

More Carols and Hymns

Want to sing an old-fashioned song about Christmas? Look it up on the Internet on The Cyber Hymnal. This site will tell you about thousands of Christian hymns and carols. Cyber Hymnal will give you the words, play the song for you, and tell you about who wrote the lyrics and music.

The Web address to this wonderful site:
http://www.cyberhymnal.org/index.htm#lk

Good King Wenceslas

Good King Wenceslas looked out on the Feast of Stephen,
When the snow lay round about, deep and crisp and even.
Brightly shone the moon that night, though the frost was cruel,
When a poor man came in sight, gathering winter fuel.

"Hither, page, and stand by me, if you know it, telling,
Yonder peasant, who is he? Where and what his dwelling?"
"Sire, he lives a good league hence, underneath the mountain,
Right against the forest fence, by Saint Agnes' fountain."

"Bring me food and bring me wine, bring me pine logs hither,
You and I will see him dine, when we bear them thither."
Page and monarch, forth they went, forth they went together,
Through the cold wind's wild lament and the bitter weather.

"Sire, the night is darker now, and the wind blows stronger,
Fails my heart, I know not how; I can go no longer."
"Mark my footsteps, my good page, tread now in them boldly,
You shall find the winter's rage freeze your blood less coldly."

In his master's steps he trod, where the snow lay dinted;
Heat was in the very sod which the saint had printed.
Therefore, Christian men, be sure, wealth or rank possessing,
You who now will bless the poor shall yourselves find blessing.

JOHN MASON NEALE

He who despises his neighbor sins,
but blessed is he who is kind to the needy.

PROVERBS 14:21

The Friendly Beasts

Jesus our brother, kind and good,
Was humbly born in a stable rude,
And the friendly beasts around Him stood;
Jesus our brother, kind and good.

"I," said the donkey, shaggy and brown,
"I carried His mother up hill and down,
I carried her safely to Bethlehem town;
I," said the donkey, shaggy and brown.

"I," said the cow, all white and red,
"I gave Him my manger for His bed,
I gave Him my hay to pillow His head;
I," said the cow, all white and red.

"I," said the sheep, with curly horn,
"I gave Him my wool for His blanket warm,
He wore my coat on Christmas morn;
I," said the sheep, with curly horn.

"I," said the dove, from the rafters high,
"Cooed Him to sleep, my mate and I,
We cooed Him to sleep, my mate and I;
I," said the dove, from the rafters high.

And every beast, by some good spell,
In the stable dark was glad to tell
Of the gift he gave Immanuel,
The gift he gave Immanuel.

TWELFTH-CENTURY CAROL

Old Carol

December, month of holly, pine, and balsam,
Of berries red, of candles' mellow light;
Of home and fireside, laughter, happy faces,
Of peace that comes upon the holy night.

EXCERPT FROM AN OLD CAROL

Hark! the Herald Angels Sing

Hark! the herald angels sing,
"Glory to the newborn King;
Peace on earth, and mercy mild,
God and sinners reconciled!"

Joyful, all ye nations rise,
Join the triumph of the skies;
With th'angelic hosts proclaim,
"Christ is born in Bethlehem!"

Hark! the herald angels sing,
"Glory to the newborn King."

CHARLES WESLEY

The wind is chill;
but let it whistle as it will.
We'll keep our Christmas
merry still.

SIR WALTER SCOTT

O Come, All Ye Faithful

O come, all ye faithful, joyful and triumphant,

O come ye, O come ye to Bethlehem;

Come and behold Him, born the King of angels;

O come, let us adore Him,

O come, let us adore Him,

O come, let us adore Him, Christ, the Lord!

JOHN FRANCIS WADE

What Child Is This?

What Child is this, Who, laid to rest,
On Mary's lap is sleeping?
Whom angels greet with anthems
    sweet,
While shepherds watch are keeping?
This, this is Christ the King,
Whom shepherds guard and angels
    sing:
This, this is Christ the King,
The Babe, the Son of Mary.

Why lies He in such mean estate,
Where ox and ass are feeding?
Good Christians, fear, for sinners
    here
The silent Word is pleading.
Nails, spear shall pierce Him through,
The cross be borne for me, for you.
Hail, hail the Word made flesh,
The Babe, the Son of Mary.

So bring Him incense, gold and myrrh,
Come peasant, king to own Him;
The King of kings salvation brings,
Let loving hearts enthrone Him.
Raise, raise a song on high,
The virgin sings her lullaby.
Joy, joy for Christ is born,
The Babe, the Son of Mary.

WILLIAM CHATTERTON DIX

Christmas—1863

I hear the bells on Christmas Day
The old familiar carols play,
And wild and sweet,
The words repeat
Of peace on earth, good-will to men.

Then from each black, accursed mouth
The cannon thundered in the South;
And with that sound
The carols drowned
Of peace on earth, good-will to men.

It was as if an earthquake rent
The hearthstones of a continent,
And made forlorn
The household born
Of peace on earth, good-will to men.

And in despair I bowed my head,
"There is no peace on earth," I said,
"For hate is strong
And mocks the song
Of peace on earth, good-will to men."

Then pealed the bells more loud and deep;
"God is not dead, nor doth He sleep;
The Wrong shall fail,
The Right prevail,
With peace on earth, good-will to men."

HENRY WADSWORTH LONGFELLOW

God Rest Ye Merry, Gentlemen

God rest ye merry, gentlemen, let nothing you dismay,
Remember Christ our Savior was born on Christmas Day;
To save us all from Satan's power when we were gone astray.

Refrain

O tidings of comfort and joy, comfort and joy;
O tidings of comfort and joy.

From God our heavenly Father a blessèd angel came;
And unto certain shepherds brought tidings of the same;
How that in Bethlehem was born the Son of God by name.

But when to Bethlehem they came where our dear Savior lay,
They found Him in a manger where oxen feed on hay;
His mother Mary kneeling unto the Lord did pray.

Now to the Lord sing praises all you within this place,
And with true love and brotherhood each other now embrace;
This holy tide of Christmas all others doth deface.

TRADITIONAL ENGLISH CAROL

Love Came Down at Christmas

Love came down at Christmas,
Love all lovely, love divine;
Love was born at Christmas,
Star and angels gave the sign.

Worship we the Godhead,
Love incarnate, love divine;
Worship we our Jesus:
But wherewith for sacred sign?

Love shall be our token,
Love shall be yours and love be mine,
Love to God and to all men,
Love for plea and gift and sign.

CHRISTINA ROSSETTI

Be Ye Glad

Then be ye glad, good people,
This night of all the year.
And light ye up your candles,
For His star it shineth clear.

CAROL

I have told you this so that you
will be filled with my joy.
Yes, your cup of joy will overflow!

JOHN 15:11 TLB

FACTS AND LEGENDS
OF CHRISTMAS JOY

Christmas When?

In approximately 350 A.D., Julian I, Bishop of Rome, ordered a large investigation of the correct birthday of Christ. He found that Western churches believed the date to be December 25, while Eastern churches believed it was January 6. Julian sided with the majority and decreed December 25 as the birthday for Christ. His decree was accepted by most churches, but the Armenians did not accept December 25 until after World War I. Prior to that, they chose to celebrate Christmas on January 6.

First English Christmas

It is believed that Christmas was first observed as a holiday in England in 521, when King Arthur celebrated his victory in reclaiming York.

Twelve Days of Christmas

During the reign of Alfred the Great, a law was passed with relation to holidays, by virtue of which the twelve days after the Nativity of our Savior were set apart for the celebration of the Christmas festival. Some writers are of opinion that, but for Alfred's strict observance of the "full twelve holy days," the Danes would not have defeated him in the year 878. It was just after the Twelfth Night that the Danish host came suddenly— "bestole," as the old Chronicle says—to Chippenham.

Christmas in the Americas

On Christmas Day, 1492, Christopher Columbus, the celebrated Genoese navigator, landed at a newly-discovered port in Cuba, which he named Navidad, because he landed there on Christmas Day.

Legend of Christmas Tree Lights

An old manuscript in a Sicilian monastery tells the following story about tree lights. When Christ was born, all the creatures of the earth, including the trees, went to Bethlehem to give Him gifts. Some trees, like the fruit-bearing ones, had much to give to Him, and they pushed the fir tree, which had nothing but its evergreen leaves, to the back. An angel felt sorry for the tree and asked some stars to come down and rest on the fir tree's boughs. When Jesus saw the lighted tree, He blessed it, and the custom of Christmas lights and ornaments began.

Legend of Christmas Tinsel

There is a legend that explains why our Christmas trees are sometimes covered with tinsel. Many years ago a godly woman trimmed her Christmas tree for her family. During the night, spiders crawled all over the tree and left their webs behind them. Jesus desired to reward the woman for all of her good deeds, so He blessed the tree, and all of the webs changed into sparkling silver threads.

Christmas Tree Lane

In Altadena, California, there is an avenue of approximately two hundred cedars named Christmas Tree Lane. Captain F. J. Woodbury planted the seeds of these trees on his ranch in the late 1800s. Each year, they are covered with ten thousand lights, and thousands of visitors come to see the beautiful sight.

First Christmas Tree Lot

In 1851 Mark Carr, a woodsman from the Catskill Mountains, set up the first Christmas-tree lot in America in New York City. He is recognized as the founder of the evergreen trade, and by the 1890s, the Catskill Mountains provided 200,000 trees for each Christmas season.

America's Christmas Tree

On December 25, 1925 the famous General Grant tree, located in King's Canyon National Park in California, was declared the Nation's Christmas Tree. This giant sequoia stands approximately 267 feet high, has a circumference of 107 feet, and is believed to be about 4,000 years old. If one were to cut it up into lumber, it would fill up twenty-eight boxcars. Many visitors come each year to attend the devotional services that are held beneath its branches on Christmas Day.

Decking the Halls for a Joyous Christmas

The idea of decorating homes on holidays is both worldwide and age-old. It is only natural that in addition to fire and trees, flowers and other plants would be used to deck the halls at a ceremony as significant as Christmas. Particularly popular in America today is the "flower of the Holy Night," representing the flaming star of Bethlehem through its red bracts and named after the United States ambassador to Mexico, Joel R. Poinsett. In 1829 he brought the plant back to his home in South Carolina, and the poinsettia's popularity at Christmas has grown ever since.

Encinitas, California, is now known as the poinsettia capital of the world because the flower is so abundant there.

Legend of the Poinsettia

Mexican legend tells that the poinsettia originated in a miracle. A poor boy, with nothing to offer Christ at the local church, fell on his knees, reassuring God how much he would like to give the gift he had no money to buy. As he stood up, there grew from the ground at his feet the first "flower of the Holy Night." He broke some of the branches with their flaming bracts and laid his gift at the altar.

Legend of Holly

Another plant often used for Christmas decoration is holly, with its pricking leaves, white flowers, and red berries. The Church developed the legend that the Cross was made of hollywood, that the sharp leaves served to form the Crown of Thorns, that the white flowers represent Christ's purity, that the bitter bark symbolizes His sorrow, and that the once yellow berries were stained red by the Lord's blood. The present scrubby appearance of what was once a fine tree can thus be explained as an eternal penance.

Bees Singing Carols?

In old England, sprays of holly were placed on beehives to wish the bees a Merry Christmas. The bees were said to hum a carol in honor of Christ.

Legend of Rosemary

Rosemary, with its fragrant gray-green leaves, used to be one of the most popular Christmas decorations and was used to adorn the boar's head at Christmas dinners. Legend holds that rosemary acquired its beautiful scent when Jesus' swaddling clothes were hung over it in the stable, and is said that its color was acquired when Mary threw her purple robe over the bush.

A City named Christmas

Five cities in the United States and one in Canada are named for the Christmas season:

> Christmas, Gila County, Arizona
> Christmas, Orange County, Florida
> Christmas, Lawrence County, Kentucky
> Christmas, Bolivar County, Mississippi
> Christmas, Roane County, Tennessee
> Christmas Island, Nova Scotia

Christmas Tip of $6,000?

In 1876 James Gordon Bennett Jr., millionaire publisher of the *New York Herald*, gave the largest Christmas tip ever recorded. After eating his Christmas breakfast at a restaurant called Delmonico's, he gave the waiter a $6,000 tip.

Saint Nicholas

Legend says that St. Nicholas was born in Patras, a city of Lycia, in Asia Minor. He was very worried about how wealthy his parents were, and when they died, he decided to secretly give away all his money.

He heard about a man who had three daughters but had no dowry for them to get married, so one night Nicholas went to the father's home and dropped a bag of gold in an open window. Soon after his good deed, the oldest daughter was married. On separate occasions, Nicholas dropped two more bags of gold in the open window for the two other daughters.

One variation of the story claims that one of the bags was dropped down the chimney and fell into one of the girls' stockings. Hence, the custom of hanging stockings for Santa Claus originated.

St. Nicholas Becomes Santa

The Dutch settlers brought a transformed St. Nicholas to the United States. His pale face became like a rosy apple. His thin frame became a plump, jolly one. His robes and pastoral staff were replaced with a red suit and hat. His old gray mare was traded in for a reindeer and sleigh.

In Europe, St. Nicholas Day has always been celebrated on December 6, and this is the day for giving presents. In the United States, St. Nicholas took over December 25, Christ's birthday.

Initially, many Protestant countries resisted the idea that St. Nicholas was the bestower of gifts, and in Germany the giver of presents has always been the Christ Child. Over time, however, the idea of Santa Claus, or St. Nicholas, has become widely accepted in many countries.

Advent

Advent is a time of preparation for the coming of Christ. The four weeks of Advent are believed to represent the four comings of Jesus: in the flesh on earth; in the hearts of Christians through the Holy Spirit; at the death of every person; and at Judgment Day. The fourth week of Advent is never completed, just as the glory of Christ's coming will never cease.

Christmas Cracker

The Christmas cracker was a party treat invented by Tom Smith and introduced to England in 1847. By 1860 he had perfected his invention that consisted of sugared almonds wrapped in twists of tissue paper. When the package was opened, it would make a loud popping noise. Different surprises, including love messages, toys, charms, jokes, and jewelry were enclosed with the almonds.

Smith tried repeatedly to sell them in seasons other than Christmas, but for some reason Christmas was when they sold the most. Christmas crackers are still used today as an integral part of some Christmas table settings.

First Christmas Seal

In 1907 the first Christmas seal in America was created by Emily Bissel who was the State Secretary of the Wilmington, Delaware, Red Cross. Proceeds from the sale of this seal were donated to a fund to fight tuberculosis. Today, more than 100 medical research facilities and charities sell Christmas seals.

First Christmas Savings Club

In 1909 Merkel Landis created the first Christmas savings club at the Carlisle Trust Company in Carlisle, Pennsylvania. It was a savings plan that allowed people to set aside money for Christmas expenses by making periodic payments throughout the year. These Christmas club accounts are still popular today.

Famous Christmas Charity

The Christmas spirit of giving is demonstrated by the annual publication of the "100 Neediest Cases" drive in the *New York Times*. Since its first appearance in 1912, this drive has raised millions of dollars for various charities and needy people.

Rudolph the Red-nosed Reindeer

The character Rudolph the red-nosed reindeer was created by Robert L. May in 1939. An advertising copywriter for Montgomery Ward Stores, May invented Rudolph for a promotional Christmas pamphlet for Ward's. Shoppers received copies of the story of a red-nosed reindeer that helped Santa Claus on Christmas Eve.

In 1947 May got the book published, and 100,000 copies were sold in the first year. In 1949 his brother-in-law, Johnny Marks, wrote the song and published it. Gene Autry, the famous cowboy singer, sang it and eventually made it one of the most popular of all Christmas songs.

*The kingdom of God is
not eating and drinking,
but righteousness and peace
and joy in the Holy Spirit.*

ROMANS 14:17 NASB

CHRISTMAS JOY
OF YESTERDAY

"Rejoice"

REJOICE, v.i. rejois'.

To experience joy and gladness in a high degree; to be exhilarated with lively and pleasurable sensations; to exult. —When the righteous are in authority, the people rejoice; but when the wicked beareth rule, the people mourn. Proverbs 29. —I will rejoice in thy salvation. Psalm 9.

WEBSTER'S 1828 *DICTIONARY OF AMERICAN ENGLISH*

First Christmas in Rome

Christians didn't generally celebrate Christ's birthday until the fourth century A.D. when the Roman celebrations of winter Saturnalia had begun seducing believers with the feasting and gift giving. Setting Christ's birthday on December 25 became one way of challenging the pagan religions, offering believers an acceptable alternative to the pagan revelry of the Romans, and sharing the Christian faith through Christian traditions.

Christmas Cake in the Time of King Arthur

In England, from earliest times, even in Roman days, it was common to bake the Yule Dough. It was generally a flat cake in the shape of a baby, which bakers presented to their customers in the same manner that chandlers presented Christmas candles.

WESTMINSTER REVIEW, 1905

The Subtleties of Christmas Joy

At medieval Christmas feasts, sugar statues were placed on the table after each course. They were called the subtleties, and they were in the form of biblical scenes, such as the Wise Men or the Nativity scene. Much ceremony and song marked the bringing in of the subtleties.

Epiphany

Epiphany is one of the oldest and most important celebrations in the Christian church. It occurs on January 6 and marks the time when the three Wise Men first saw the Christ Child. The arrival of the three Wise Men at the stable on this night, the Twelfth Night, was long remembered with a party.

The Twelfth Night cake was baked in honor of the Magi. It contained a bean and a pea, and whoever found them played king and queen for the rest of the evening, ordering all sorts of games to be played. In England, the tradition of this cake dates back as early as the medieval court of King Edward II.

Monograms of the Wise Men

In the old days in countries like Germany, Poland, Czechoslovakia, Switzerland, and Sweden, people used to write "C+M+B"—the initials of the three Wise Men—over the doors of their homes.

Early Irish Christmas

In 1158 King Henry II of England, celebrating the Christmas festival at Worcester, took the crown from his head and placed it upon the altar, after which he never wore it. He did not cease to keep Christmas, however. In 1171 he went to Ireland, where the chiefs of the land displayed a wonderful alacrity in taking the oath of allegiance and were rewarded by being entertained in a style that astonished them.

Finding no place in Dublin large enough to contain his own followers, much less his guests, Henry had a house built in Irish fashion, of twigs and wattles, in the village of Hogges. There he held high revelry during Christmastide, teaching his subjects to eat cranes' flesh and take their part in miracle plays, masques, mummeries, and tournaments. A great number of oxen were roasted so that all the people might take part in the rejoicings.

King Henry Remembers the Poor

At one Christmas celebration, King Henry III of England had over 600 oxen slaughtered for the feast. Yet although he feasted the rich, he did not forget the poor. When he kept his Christmas at Winchester in 1248, he ordered his treasurer to fill Westminster Hall with poor people and feast them there for a week.

Christmas Tree

Over time, the yule log has been replaced by the Christmas tree, which became popular as the cities began to grow. A spruce or fir, decked with baubles, bangles, and lights, has been the centerpiece of the celebration, and the tree symbolizes Christ bringing new life to the earth after the long, dark days of winter. In 1604 in Strasbourg, the first Christmas tree appears in literature.

The most popular tradition, however, insists that the first Christmas tree was cut down by Martin Luther, who brought it home and decorated it with candles to imitate "the starry skies of Bethlehem that Holy Night." Under it, Luther put a crèche and figures of Joseph, Mary, the Baby Jesus, and various animals.

Upside Down Christmas

In some poorer communities, it was initially customary to hang the Christmas tree from the ceiling, often upside down.

First Christmas Tree Decorations

Christmas trees were initially decorated with nuts, fruit, gingerbread, candy, and paper decorations. Candles were first mentioned as decorations for a tree in Germany in 1737. There is a story that at this time a woman lit candles on or around little trees for her children and placed presents beneath each tree.

Hot-Cockles

The English played a Christmas game called Hot-cockles. One blindfolded person would kneel or lie face down in the middle of the room. The other people would take turns tapping the blindfolded person on the shoulder, while he or she would guess their names. When the person guessed correctly, the person whose identity had been discovered would be blindfolded to begin the game again.

A letter dated December 28, 1711 appeared in the *Spectator* regarding this game:

> Mr. Spectator, I am a Footman in a great Family and am in Love with the House-maid. We were all at Hot-cockles last Night in the Hall these Holidays; when I lay down and was blinded, she pull'd off her Shoe, and hit me with the Heel such a Rap, as almost broke my Head to Pieces. Pray, Sir, was this Love or Spite?

Hot Cereal on Christmas Morning

It used to be tradition to eat frumenty the first thing on Christmas morning in many parts of England. Frumenty consisted of wheat that was slowly stewed in milk, and it was served with raisins, sugar, and spices.

Nine-Foot Mince Pie

The most famous mince pie in the annals of Christmas was one served at Sir Henry Grey's in London in 1770. It was nine feet in circumference, weighed 165 pounds, and was pushed into the dining hall on a four-wheel cart.

In this pie were four geese, four wild ducks, two woodcocks, two "turkies," four partridges, seven blackbirds, six pigeons, two rabbits, two neat's tongues, two bushels of flour, twenty pounds of butter, and sundry items. It is no small wonder then that there is a southwestern English saying: "The Devil himself dare not appear in Cornwall during Christmas for fear of being baked in a pie."

Plum Pudding with No Plums

Plum pudding is a traditional English Christmas dish that appeared around 1670. Ironically, there are no plums in plum pudding. "Plum" could refer to raisins in the pudding, or it could be related to the ingredients swelling when they bake. Originally, plum pudding consisted of porridge with pieces of meat, dried fruit like raisins and currants, rum, brandy, butter, sugar, eggs, and various spices.

Usually, the entire family oversaw the making of the pudding. Each person took turns stirring the mix while making a wish. A coin, a thimble, a button, and a ring were added to the pudding. As the family ate, each object meant something to the person who found it: the coin represented wealth for the coming year, the button symbolized bachelorhood, the thimble stood for spinsterhood, and the ring represented marriage.

Largest Plum Pudding Ever!

The largest plum pudding ever recorded was created in the small town of Paignton in Devon, England, in 1819. It was customary for this village to make a huge plum pudding for the entire town once every fifty years.

Although this custom is no longer practiced, in 1819 the pudding contained four hundredweights of flour, 120 pounds of suet (fat), and 120 pounds of raisins. The final creation weighed 900 pounds and was pulled by three horses.

First English Christmas in America

The first English Christmas in America occurred at Jamestown, Virginia, in 1607. Captain John Smith wrote the following about the experience:

"The extreme winds, rayne, frost and snow caused us to keep Christmas among the savages where we were never more merry, nor fed on more plenty of good Oysters, Fish, Flesh, Wildfowl and good bread, nor never had better fires in England."

Christmas River Crossing

In 1776 American colonials did not participate in Christmas celebrations because of the strong Puritan influence at that time. The Hessians, however, who were German soldiers hired by the British, did celebrate the holiday.

On Christmas night of that year, George Washington crossed the Delaware River and caught the Hessians, who were busy with their Christmas celebrations, by surprise. This initial action by Washington led to a later victory at the Battle of Trenton, America's first big victory in the Revolutionary War.

The American Christmas Turkey

The American tradition of eating turkey at Christmas time did not begin until the seventeenth century. Prior to that, a much more common dish served at Christmas, especially in England, was the boar's head. It was considered to be a delicacy, and it was served with great pride. A garland of rosemary and laurel was pressed on the boar's head, and a lemon was placed in its mouth.

Over time, this main dish was replaced by pickled swine's flesh, roast beef, capon, goose, and the American turkey.

Knickerbocker Christmas

In 1809 Washington Irving, writing under the pseudonym "Dietrich Knickerbocker," was the first to refer to the custom of hanging stockings in *Knickerbocker History of New York*. He wrote about "hanging up a stocking on the chimney on St. Nicholas eve; which stocking is always found in the morning miraculously filled—for the good St. Nicholas has ever been a great giver of gifts."

Andrew Jackson's White House Stocking

President Andrew Jackson's niece Mary Donelson and several other children came to celebrate Christmas at the White House in 1835. On Christmas Eve the President had the children come to his room and invited them to hang their stockings. One of the children suggested that Jackson should have a stocking as well. Jackson relented, telling the children that he had waited nearly seventy years to put up a stocking.

Royal English Christmas Tree

When Queen Victoria married the German-born Prince Albert, he put a Christmas tree up in Windsor Castle in 1841 and officially brought the Christmas tree tradition to England. Seven years later, in 1848, the *Illustrated London News* described their eight-foot fir tree with its six tiers of branches:

> On each tier, or branch, are arranged a dozen wax tapers. Pendent from the branches are elegant trays, baskets, bonbonnières, and other receptacles for sweetmeats, of the most varied and expensive kind; and of all forms, colours, and degrees of beauty. Fancy cakes, gilt gingerbread and eggs filled with sweetmeats, are also suspended by variously-coloured ribbons from the branches.

Pay to View a Christmas Tree

"Christmas tree" appeared in print for the first time in a York, Pennsylvania, paper in 1830. The Dorcas Society of York, a ladies' charity group, published a notice in the paper inviting people to attend an exhibition of various articles along with a famous Christmas tree. The tickets to this event cost six and a quarter cents.

Christmas in the White House

In 1805 Thomas Jefferson celebrated Christmas with one hundred guests, including his six grandchildren, by playing a merry jig on his fiddle. In 1835 President Andrew Jackson had his chef make various ice shapes for his Christmas party. One of them was a small, frosted pine tree with toy animals around it.

In 1856 Franklin Pierce had the first White House Christmas tree. In 1895 Grover Cleveland became the first president to use electric lights on the White House tree. In 1923 Calvin Coolidge started the tradition of lighting a tree on the White House lawn.

In 1953 Dwight D. Eisenhower decided to send the first official presidential Christmas card, and he asked an old friend, Joyce C. Hall, founder of Hallmark Cards, Inc., for help. Since then, Hallmark has published official presidential Christmas cards for every president.

Christmas Cards

An Englishman, J. C. Horsley, supposedly designed the first formal Christmas card in 1843. It was lithographed on stiff, dark cardboard and depicted, in colors, a party of grown-ups and children with glasses of wine raised in a toast over the words "A Merry Christmas and a Happy New Year to you." One thousand of these cards were printed. Today, over a billion cards are sold each year in Britain and the United States alone.

Eating Christmas Tree Leftovers!

In the Victorian era, popcorn and cranberry were often strung together and used as decorations for the Christmas tree. Also, the tree was often adorned with sweetmeats and fruits. These treats remained untouched until the dismantling of the tree after the Twelfth Night. Then, they could be eaten. Thus, the day of dismantling the tree, which is so sad for children today, was the exciting culmination of the Christmas celebration in that time period.

First Christmas Lights

Around 1895 Ralph E. Morris, an employee of the New England Telephone and Telegraph Company, collected twelve-volt flashlight size bulbs used for telephone switchboards, and he transformed them into a string of electric lights for his family's Christmas tree.

Christ, the Light of the World

Candles and lights have long been associated with the Christmas tree. Perhaps following the lead of the Jews, who celebrate their Hanukkah, or Feast of the Lights, in December. Medieval Church custom identified the candle with Christ, the Light of the World. At Christmastime candles are often placed around the house, in the windows, and on the tree.

"I am the light of the world.
Whoever follows me will never walk in darkness,
but will have the light of life."

JOHN 8:12

First Community Christmas Tree

Originally, Christmas trees were only used within the home. The first community Christmas tree in the United States was erected in Madison Square Garden, New York, in 1912.

History of the Candy Cane

In the late 1800s, a candy maker in Indiana wanted to express the meaning of Christmas through a symbol made of candy. He bent one of his white candy sticks into the shape of a candy cane and incorporated symbols of Christ's love and sacrifice. First, he used a white peppermint stick. The color white symbolizes the purity of Jesus.

Next, he added three small stripes to symbolize the pain inflicted upon Jesus before his death on the cross. He added a bold stripe to represent the blood Jesus shed for mankind.

With the crook on top, it looks like a shepherd's staff, because Jesus is the shepherd of man. Upside down, it becomes the letter "J," symbolizing the first letter in Jesus' name. The candy maker wanted everyone to remember what Christmas is really all about.

World War I Christmas Peace

During World War I on Christmas Day in 1915, the Germans set aside their rifles and walked into the no man's land territory. They carried food and began to sing Christmas carols.

In absolute shock, the British soldiers recognized the tunes of the familiar carols. They began to sing with them. The men sang the carols together in both German and English. They ate and sang together until their officers eventually split them up and refused to allow them to fraternize with the enemy.

A Big Christmas Thank-you

Each year the people of Oslo, Norway, send a Christmas tree to the British people, and it is set up in the center of London in Trafalgar Square. It is sent in memory of a difficult time during World War II when the Norwegian king was in exile from his German-occupied country.

During each year of his exile, a tree from Norway was smuggled past the Germans and delivered to him in England. Since 1947, Norway has sent this yearly tree to the British people in remembrance for their kindness to their previous king.

Manger in a Walnut Ornaments

One European Christmas tradition involved painting nuts in silver or gold and hanging them on the tree. Oftentimes, a scripture or tiny manger scene was placed in a hollowed-out walnut. The walnut usually had been broken in half and was hinged on one side so that one could easily open and close it to enjoy what was nestled inside.

*I say these things in the world
so that they might have my joy
in their hearts, in all its fullness.*

JOHN 17:13 TEV

CHRISTMAS JOY IN OTHER LANDS

"Merry Christmas" Greetings in Other Countries:

Bulgaria	*Chestita Koleda*
Croatia	*Sretan Bozic*
Finland	*Houska Joulua*
France	*Joyeux Noël*
Germany	*Froehliche Weihnachten*
Italy	*Buone Feste Natalizie*
Portugal	*Boas Festas*
Spain	*Feliz Navidad*

Christmas in Australia

One Australian Christmas tradition is the singing of carols by large crowds of people carrying torches and candles. Special candles are sold in stores, and all of the proceeds go to various charities.

In Melbourne, this tradition began in 1937, and is called "Carols by Candlelight." It attracts around 150,000 people and raises about that many dollars to donate to the charities.

At nighttime the candles are lit, and the carolers walk toward a stage by the Yarra River. The hand-held candles illuminate the whole park, and the carols are sung until midnight, when the evening culminates in a chorus of "Auld Lang Syne."

Christmas Food in Austria

In Austria, characteristic foods of Christmas are: *Fruchtbrod,* made of raisins, currants, chopped figs and dates and made into a cake which is served hot; chopped and baked carp; beef, vegetables and beer.

Christmas in Belgium

In each village in Flanders, it is a Christmas tradition to assign three men to walk along the streets dressed as the three Wise Men.

In order to be selected for this honor, the men must have been extremely virtuous the preceding year. These three men walk the streets and sing two songs at every home in the village.

One of the songs describes the journey of the three Wise Men. The other song is a version of "O Tannenbaum." After singing their songs, the men are usually offered cups of tea or pancakes.

Christmas in Brazil

In Brazil, many people express the lesson that giving, not receiving, is the real spirit of Christmas. Oftentimes, people bring small gifts of food, wrapped in white paper, to the front of the church. The gifts are placed around a small manger filled with straw and a little light, representing Jesus as the "Light of the World." These gifts enable poorer families to prepare their own Christmas dinners.

Christmas in England

In England, December 26 is known as Boxing Day. Centuries ago on the day after Christmas, it was the custom to give Christmas boxes to servants and people who performed public services, such as mailmen, policemen, milkmen, and others. The boxes contained money given as gratitude for the services rendered. This tradition still carries on today in the form of Christmas bonuses for employees.

Christmas in France

In France, the Great Supper is a meal that is served after Midnight Mass in many areas of France. This meal consists of thirteen different foods that represent Jesus and His twelve disciples. In place of a Christmas cake, a *Bûche de Noël,* or chocolate Christmas log is served in honor of the Yule log tradition. It is a light chocolate cake rolled with cream, liqueur, and nuts. It is then covered with chocolate icing and powdered sugar, and it is decorated with a candle.

Italian Christmas Ceppo

One Christmas tradition in Italy is the *ceppo,* which is a pyramid-shaped frame with several shelves. The *ceppo* is decorated with greenery, ribbons, candles, and other Christmas accessories. Presents, cookies, and candy are placed on the shelves. Sometimes the Nativity scene, or *presepio,* is also placed on one of the shelves. Oftentimes, the *ceppo* is motorized so that it revolves.

Christmas in Lithuania

In Lithuania, the Christmas Eve dinner table is covered with straw in memory of Jesus' birth. Then, an unconsecrated wafer, which represents the love and harmony of the Christmas season, is shared by all the family members.

Christmas in Mexico

In Mexico, the home must be decorated for Christmas by December 16—the beginning of the Mexican *posadas*. This word means resting place or inn and is used to describe the custom in which people, some acting like Mary and Joseph and others acting like the cruel innkeepers, travel from house to house in a dramatic re-creation of the Holy Family's difficult search for shelter. The *posadas* last for nine days, the same period of time that tradition says Joseph and Mary searched for a place to stay. Each evening, the procession culminates in a party complete with dancing and singing.

Christmas in the Philippines

In the Philippines, one common Christmas tradition involves the performing of plays called *pastores*. People travel from town to town to act out these plays that portray important events from the Bible.

On the Way to Bethlehem

There is a Spanish legend that each year Three Kings cross Spain on their way to Bethlehem and leave gifts for all the children who have been well behaved. On Epiphany Eve, the Spanish children put out carrot- and hay-filled shoes for the camels of the Kings.

*You will rejoice,
and no one will
take away your joy.*

JOHN 16:22

Making Your
Christmas Joyful

Giving Away Christmas Cheer

Increase your Christmas joy by giving it away. Invite those who will be alone for Christmas into your home for the holiday season. Or celebrate Christmas a day early and spend Christmas Day helping out at a soup kitchen serving meals for the homeless. You can also arrange to buy gifts anonymously for someone at church who cannot afford gifts.

Try these simple gestures and others to experience the kind of joy God had when He sent the greatest Gift of all.

Easy Turkey Dressing

1 8-ounce package cornbread dressing mix
1 8-ounce package herb bread dressing mix
1 cup chopped celery
½ to 1 cup chopped onion

Follow the directions on the dressing mixes regarding amounts of water and butter. Put water and butter into a large saucepan on medium heat. When it comes to a boil, add the chopped celery and onion. Simmer until softened, about 5-10 minutes. Put dressing mix into a large bowl. Pour the liquid mixture over it and gently toss.

Pour all of this into an 8½ x 11 inch baking dish. Bake uncovered at 325 degrees for one hour. This recipe can be made the day before and kept in the refrigerator until time to bake, thereby reducing the stress of the day and increasing the Christmas joy of the cook!

Increase Your Christmas Joy

Christmas stress interfering with Christmas Joy? Try these time-saving hints to bounce back and celebrate.

1. Use Christmas decorated bags instead of wrapping every gift with paper.

2. Shop on the Internet for out-of-state relatives—Internet companies will wrap, include your personal note, and mail your gift for you.

3. Send your Christmas letters and cards by e-mail.

4. Get others involved. Send teenagers to the mall on gift quests for younger siblings. Assign the family writer the task of writing the Christmas letter. Set other family members to baking in the weeks before Christmas and freeze goodies ahead of time.

It's Beginning to Smell a Lot like Christmas!

Use a potpourri of cinnamon or evergreen to scent the house with Christmas cheer! Add Christmas music in the background to complete that Christmas atmosphere.

Mustard Sauce for Christmas Ham

1 can (1¾ ounces) dry mustard
6¼ ounces vinegar
2 beaten eggs
1 cup sugar

Put dry mustard in measuring cup and add vinegar until it reaches one cup. Stir well and let sit overnight. Then, add two beaten eggs and one cup of sugar. Cook over medium heat and stir until thick.

Christmas Cookies

1½ cups sifted confectioner's sugar
1 cup butter
1 egg
1 teaspoon vanilla

½ teaspoon almond flavoring
2½ cups flour
1 teaspoon baking soda
1 teaspoon cream of tartar

Cream sugar and butter. Mix in egg and flavorings. Measure flour. Blend dry ingredients; stir in. Refrigerate dough for two to three hours.

Heat oven to 375 degrees. Divide ½ of the dough and roll it out on a lightly floured pastry cloth until it is ¼ inch thick. Use Christmas cookie cutters to cut out the cookies.

(continued next page)

Sprinkle the cookies with sugar and then bake them, or bake them first and then frost them once they are cooled. Place cookies on a lightly greased baking sheet, and bake for 7 to 8 minutes.

This recipe makes approximately five dozen cookies.

Icing for Christmas Cookies

1 cup sifted confectioner's sugar   ½ teaspoon vanilla
¼ teaspoon salt   1 tablespoon water

Mix all of the ingredients. Tint, if desired, with food coloring.

Christmas Joy Across the Miles

Keep Christmas joy in high flight even if a special loved one is going to be far away for Christmas. Have a family meeting and videotape the gift-wrapping and box-packing for the loved one complete with special close-ups of family members sending Christmas greetings and special family news.

A digital camera can capture special holiday pictures to send by e-mail. Collect enough to send one or two each day of the Christmas season.

Child-Friendly Christmas

Do you have children on your Christmas horizon? Make their Christmas extra joyful by creating a child friendly environment. Decorate in Christmas theme using small stuffed Christmas animals and disposable paper decorations. If a child wants to pick up an item or to take an item home, be prepared to say a cheerful, "Yes!"

If children are visiting, make sure there are areas near the adult fun where they can spread out their games and building blocks. Have a special table set up for puzzles and coloring.

Use gift bags so children have something with handles in which to carry Christmas toys. These will help in tidying things up before dinner and bedtime as well.

Have a special Christmas video ready for each day.

Bake those sugar cookies, but save frosting them for your little visitors. Turn them loose in the kitchen with colored frostings, sprinkles, and plastic knives to decorate the official Christmas cookies. Display them on the kitchen counter on a special plate for all to see.

Use battery-run candles on tables and in windows for safety and to eliminate one more "no!" item.

Sweet Rolls for Christmas Morning

2 loaves frozen bread dough—thawed

½ cup sugar

1 teaspoon cinnamon

½ cup white sugar

½ cup brown sugar

1 stick butter

¾ cup vanilla ice cream

(continued on next page)

Break up one loaf of the thawed bread into bite-sized pieces, and place them into a greased bundt pan.

Sprinkle with cinnamon and ½ cup white sugar. Then, bring white sugar, brown sugar, butter, and ice cream to a boil for two minutes. Pour mixture over the cut up dough pieces.

Break up the second loaf of thawed bread into bite-sized pieces, and layer on top of the other dough. Let rise until doubles.

Bake at 350 degrees for 45 minutes. Let it stand for 10 minutes before serving.

A Year of Christmas Joy for Shut-ins

Got someone special in a nursing home or retirement community? Buy an attractive twelve-month calendar with pockets. Fill each month with treats and include a sealed greeting card for each holiday of the year.

Suggested items are bookmarks, sealed tea bags, notepads, pens, special poems, compact disks of favorite music, photos of grandchildren or important events, a decorative handkerchief, lapel pins, very small inspirational books, and stationery.

Since mail is often rare for shut-ins, why not subscribe to an inspirational magazine like *Guideposts* or *Readers Digest* as well?

Extend the Life of Your Christmas Tree

After the Christmas season is over, consider finding various ways to get the most out of your Christmas tree. For example, put your tree in your backyard and cover it with peanut butter, seeds, and orange slices. Your Christmas tree will be transformed into a giant bird feeder, one that not only feeds the birds, but also provides them with needed protection against the cold and wind. Or, if you would prefer, cut your tree into smaller pieces to use as logs for your fireplace.

In the Bleak Midwinter

In the bleak midwinter, frosty wind made moan,
Earth stood hard as iron, water like a stone;
Snow had fallen, snow on snow, snow on snow,
In the bleak midwinter, long ago.

Our God, heaven cannot hold Him, nor earth sustain;
Heaven and earth shall flee away when He comes to reign.
In the bleak midwinter a stable place sufficed
The Lord God Almighty, Jesus Christ.

Enough for Him, Whom cherubim, worship night and day,
Breastful of milk, and a mangerful of hay;
Enough for Him, Whom angels fall before,
The ox and ass and camel which adore.

Angels and archangels may have gathered there,
Cherubim and seraphim thronged the air;
But His mother only, in her maiden bliss,
Worshipped the beloved with a kiss.

What can I give Him, poor as I am?
If I were a shepherd, I would bring a lamb;
If I were a Wise Man, I would do my part;
Yet what I can give Him: give my heart.

CHRISTINA ROSSETTI

References

* (p. 8-9,50-1,55,57,58-9,62-3) *Cyber Hymnal,* WebPage. (Website: http://www.cyber-hymnal.org.) * (pp. 12,60-1) Robert Lohan, *Christmas Tales for Reading Aloud* (New York: Stephen Daye Press, 1946). * (p. 13) Matthew Henry's Concise Commentary on the Whole Bible * (p. 15) John Chrysostom, "Homilies on Matthew," *Early Church Fathers* (Version 2.0), volume 10. Christian Classics Ethereal Library, (Grand Rapids Michigan: CCEL, 2001) *(pp. 17, 21) *Norman Rockwell's Christmas Book,* Lena Tabori Fried and Ruth Eisenstein, eds. (New York: Harry N. Abrams, Inc., 1977). * (p. 19) Eugene Field, *Christmas Tales and Christmas Verse,* 1912. *(pp. 15) Elva Sophronia Smith, *Christmas in Legend and Story: a Book for Boys and Girls* (Freeport, New York: Books for Libraries Press, 1915). * (pp. 20,24,41,68,75,82,83,94,95,101,104,111, 114,130) Alfred Carl Hottes, *1001 Christmas Facts and Fancies* (New York: A. T. De La Mare Company, Inc., 1937). *(p. 25) Meynell, Alice. The Poems of Alice Meynell (1923). E-text. http://poetry.elcore.net/Catholic Poets/Meynell. * (pp. 23,72,74,75,81,86, 112,113,116,155) Irena Chalmers, *The Great American Christmas Almanac* (New York: Viking Penguin Inc., 1988). * (pp. 28-9,31,34-35,40) Eugene Field, *The Poems of Eugene Field, Complete Edition* (New York: Charles Scribner's Sons, 1913). * (pp. 26,70,71,98-9,100) W. F. Dawson, *Christmas: Its Origin and Associations* (London: Elliot Stock, 1902). * (pp. 27,52-3,64) *The Miracle of Christmas,* William R. Webb, ed. (Kansas City, Missouri: Hallmark Cards, Inc., 1966). * (p. 33)Alfred Domett, "A Christmas Hymn," Stevenson, Burton Egbert (ed) *The Home Book of Verse: American and English,* 3rd Ed., Henry Holt and Co., New York, 1918, Online version, n. p. * (p. 36) John Bartlett, *Familiar Quotations*

(Garden City, New York: Garden City Publishing Co., Inc., 1944) p. 653. * (p. 37) *A Christmas Sampler,* Maryjane Hooper Tonn, ed. (Milwaukee: Ideals Publishing Corporation, 1974) p. 80. * (44) "Isaac Watts," *Cyber Hymnal,* WebPage, (Website: http://www.cyber-hymnal.org.) * (45) "Antioch" *Cyber Hymnal,* WebPage, (Website: http://www.cyberhym-nal.org.).* (pp. 38,39,41,54,65,78,125,139) *The Book of Christmas* (Capetown: The Reader's Digest Association, Inc., 1985). * (pp. 48,118,129) William Sansom, *A Book of Christmas* (New York: McGraw-Hill Book Company, 1968). * (pp. 69,73,80,128,131,132, 133,136,137,138) Herbert H. Wernecke, *Christmas Customs around the World* (Philadelphia: The Westminster Press, 1975). * (pp. 74,114,115,116,118, 119) Daniel J. Foley, *The Christmas Tree; an Evergreen Garland Filled with History, Folklore, Symbolism, Traditions, Legends and Stories* (Philadelphia: Chilton Company, 1960). * (pp. 76,77,78,101,106,117, 120) Tristram Potter Coffin, *The Illustrated Book of Christmas Folklore* (1922). * (pp. 79,84,85,96,97,102,103, 121,134,137) *A Celebration of Christmas,* Gillian Cooke, ed. (New York: G. P. Putnams's Sons, 1980). * (pp. 76,87,88,89,100,105, 107,108,109,110,123,124,134,135) Gerard and Patricia Del Re, *The Christmas Almanack* (Garden City, New York: Doubleday & Company, Inc., 1979). * (pp.122) *Merry Christmas: Inspiring Quotes, Poems, and Stories to Celebrate the Season* (Tulsa, Oklahoma: Honor Books) pp. 78-79. * (p. 130) "What the Different Nationalities Eat at Christmas, *Harper's Weekly,* December 31, 1910. * (p. 143,146) Recipe from JoEllen Louis. * (p. 147-8) Recipe from Lisa Hughes. * (p. 152-3) Recipe from Janelle Zander. * (p. 156) Rossetti, Christina, "In the Bleak Midwinter," *Cyber Hymnal,* WebPage. (Website: http://www.cyberhymnal.org.).

Additional copies of this book and other Christmas titles from Honor Books are available from your local bookstore.

Jesus: the Reason for the Season
Christmas Is
Merry Christmas
Christmas Treasures from the Heart
The Greatest Christmas Ever

If you have enjoyed this book, or if it has impacted your life, we would like to hear from you.

Please contact us at:

Honor Books
Department E
P.O. Box 55388
Tulsa, Oklahoma 74155

Or by e-mail at

info@honorbooks.com